Enhancing Environmental Justice in EPA Permitting Programs

APRIL 2011

**A Report of Advice and Recommendations
of the
National Environmental Justice Advisory Council**

A Federal Advisory Committee to the U.S. Environmental Protection Agency

ACKNOWLEDGEMENTS

The National Environmental Justice Advisory Council (NEJAC) acknowledges the efforts of the Permitting Subgroup in preparing the initial draft of this report. The members of the Subgroup are listed on page 2 of this report. The NEJAC also acknowledges the staff of EPA's Office of Environmental Justice, especially Victoria Robinson, NEJAC Designated Federal Officer, and APEX Direct, Inc, which provided contractor support.

DISCLAIMER

TABLE OF CONTENTS

APPENDICES

NATIONAL ENVIRONMENTAL JUSTICE ADVISORY COUNCIL

Members:
Don Aragon
Chuck Barlow
Teri Blanton
Sue Briggum
M. Kathryn Brown
Peter Captain, Sr.
Jolene Catron
Wynecta Fisher
Stephanie Hall
Jodena Henneke
Savanala 'Savi' Horne
Hilton Kelley
Langdon Marsh
Margaret May
Vernice Miller-Travis
Paul Mohai
Vien T. Nguyen
Edith Pestana
Shankar Prasad
John Ridgway
Nia Robinson
Patricia Salkin
Nicholas Targ
Kimberly Wasserman

April 30, 2011

Lisa P. Jackson
Administrator
U.S. Environmental Protection Agency
1200 Pennsylvania Avenue, NW
Washington, D.C. 20460

Dear Administrator Jackson:

The National Environmental Justice Advisory Council (NEJAC) is pleased to submit the report, *Enhancing Environmental Justice in EPA Permitting Programs*, for the Agency's review. This report contains advice and recommendations about how the Agency can most effectively enhance environmental justice throughout its permitting programs. The advice is to be considered both in terms of the environmental permits that EPA issues and those permits issued by the states and tribes under delegation of authority or federal oversight of state and tribal programs. Although EPA's charge to the Council focused on "types" of permits, the Council's response respectfully shifts the focus to a broader context: cumulative impacts from multiple permits and environmental conditions. Prioritizing environmental justice opportunities by traditional permit type is too narrow to properly address the charge. Thus, this report addresses a broader approach.

The following is the list of key recommendations proposed by the NEJAC:

- Cumulative environmental impacts, permitted or not, must be addressed and mitigated within existing and new permits, regardless of permit type.

- Permitting covers a broad range of regulatory work, including renewals, modifications, enforcement actions, and settlements. All of these permit-related processes have important elements for environmental justice engagement. This is not just about new facilities and their permit applications.

- Formal agreements between EPA regions and their respective delegated or authorized states, tribes, and/or other jurisdictions need to have environmental justice addressed more – both in general and with specific actions and noted responsibilities. Multiple ideas and examples are provided.

- More recent permit issues related to hydraulic fracturing and mountain top mining need immediate review from an environmental justice perspective. Acknowledging several prior Council reports to EPA related to permitting over the past 15 years (cited in footnotes), this report draws attention to newer permit related challenges in need of environmental justice attention and action by EPA and others.

A Federal Advisory Committee to the U.S. Environmental Protection Agency

- Permits from other federal agencies need environmental justice review and support from EPA and the Interagency Working Group on Environmental Justice. Examples include: U.S. Army Corps of Engineers Section 404 permits; U.S. Department of Defense clean-up work on Formally Used Defense Sites; and U.S. Department of Interior environmental work/oversight in Indian Country.

Once again, thank you for this opportunity to provide recommendations for enhancing environmental justice in EPA's permitting programs.

Sincerely,

Elizabeth Le Yeampierre

Elizabeth Yeampierre
Chair

cc: NEJAC Members
Lisa Garcia, Senior Policy Advisor to the Administrator for Environmental Justice
Charles Lee, Director, Office of Environmental Justice (OEJ)
Victoria Robinson, NEJAC DFO, OEJ

ENHANCING ENVIRONMENTAL JUSTICE IN EPA PERMITTING PROGRAMS

A Report of Advice and Recommendations of the National Environmental Justice Advisory Council

1.0 INTRODUCTION

1.1 The Charge and Timeline.

At the July 2010 meeting of the National Environmental Justice Advisory Council (NEJAC or the Council), the U.S. Environmental Protection Agency (EPA) asked the Council for advice about how to enhance environmental justice throughout its permitting programs. The advice is to be considered both in terms of the environmental permits that EPA issues and those permits issued by the states and tribes under delegation of authority or federal oversight of state and tribal programs. The Council was given a charge to develop answers to two questions:

- Question #1 – What types of EPA-issued permits should EPA focus on now, to work on incorporating environmental justice concerns into EPA's permits?
- Question #2 – What types of permits issued pursuant to federal environmental laws, whether they are federal, state, or tribal permits, are best suited for exploring and addressing the complex issue of cumulative impacts? Such impacts come from exposure to multiple sources and existing conditions that are critical to the effective consideration of environmental justice in permitting.

A Subgroup of the Council was assembled to address these questions in August 2010. The Subgroup quickly determined that a preliminary response to the charge questions was needed and would be discussed at the November 2010 NEJAC meeting. To conduct its work, the Subgroup was provided the opportunity for six one-hour calls, one of which took place as part of a public conference call addressing several topics. The Subgroup has endeavored to be responsive to EPA's desire to proceed expeditiously on this important programmatic goal. However, the Subgroup notes that the timeline for deliberations was too short. Scheduling did not allow face-to-face meetings or the kinds of sustained deliberation that have been the hallmark of NEJAC work products produced after a six-month to two-year effort, typical for substantive NEJAC reports.

At the November 2010 Council meeting in Kansas City, Missouri, the Subgroup presented its findings and draft report to the full Council. After deliberations, all Council members were able to provide input and draft refinements. The Council adopted this report as final in early 2011.

1.2 The Subgroup

The Subgroup's work was chaired by Mr. John Ridgway and facilitated by the Council's Designated Federal Officer, Ms. Victoria Robinson. Administrative and document production assistance to the Subgroup was provided by APEX Direct, Inc., EPA's support contractor for the NEJAC. The members of the Subgroup – and the stakeholder categories they represent – are listed in Exhibit 1.

2.0   SUMMARY

This report outlines many opportunities for EPA to enhance environmental justice through, and related to, permitting. Although EPA's charge to the Council focused on "types" of permits, the Council's response respectfully shifted the focus to a broader context: cumulative impacts from multiple permits and environmental conditions. Prioritizing environmental justice opportunities by traditional permit type is too narrow to properly address the charge. Thus, this report addresses a broader approach.

Key recommendations include the following:

- Cumulative environmental impacts, permitted or not, must be addressed and mitigated within existing and new permits, regardless of permit type.

- Permitting covers a broad range of regulatory work, including renewals, modifications, enforcement actions, and settlements. All of these permit-related processes have important elements for environmental justice engagement. This is not just about new facilities and their permit applications.

- Formal agreements between EPA regions and their respective delegated or authorized states, tribes, and/or other jurisdictions need to have environmental justice addressed more – both in general and with specific actions and noted responsibilities. Multiple ideas and examples are provided.

- More recent permit issues related to hydraulic fracturing and mountain top mining need immediate review from an environmental justice perspective. Acknowledging several prior Council reports to EPA related to permitting over the past 15 years (cited in footnotes), this report draws attention to newer permit related challenges in need of environmental justice attention and action by EPA and others.

- Permits from other federal agencies need environmental justice review and support from EPA and the Interagency Working Group on Environmental Justice. Examples include: U.S. Army Corps of Engineers Section 404 permits; U.S. Department of Defense clean-up work on Formally Used Defense Sites; and U.S. Department of Interior environmental work/oversight in Indian Country.

This report is an initial response to EPA's questions to the NEJAC regarding environmental justice and permitting. Although broad in its considerations, the report was prepared in an unusually short time, lacking expertise and resources. If EPA desires more advice or detail from the Council on this topic, a work group should be established, more time will be needed, and input from regions and delegated or authorized state and tribal entities is required.

Exhibit 1
MEMBERS OF NEJAC ENVIRONMENTAL JUSTICE IN PERMITTING SUBGROUP

Mr. John Ridgway, *Chair*	State/Local Government
Mr. Don Aragon	Tribal Governments & Indigenous Organization
Ms. Sue Briggum	Business/Industry
Ms. Jodena Henneke	Business/Industry
Mr. Hilton Kelley	Community-based Organization
Ms. Vernice Miller-Travis	Non-governmental Organization
Ms. Edith Pestana	State/Local Government
Dr. Shankar Prasad	Non-governmental Organization

3.0 GENERAL CONSIDERATIONS AND RECOMMENDATIONS REGARDING ENVIRONMENTAL JUSTICE IN PERMITTING

3.1 Important Caveat

This report only addresses the most basic and cursory elements of EPA's charge to the NEJAC. Informed advice on this complex subject demands close interaction between EPA staff and the NEJAC in order to leverage a wide breadth of knowledge and experience, and then to find consensus positions on how EPA should proceed.

Recommendation:

1. Establish a formal NEJAC Work Group on Permitting and Environmental Justice to bring in the needed expertise and allow adequate time for good recommendations.

3.2 Potential Coverage of EPA's New Environmental Justice in Permitting Initiative

To put EPA's request in context and understand the impact of selecting one or more categories of environmental permits, the NEJAC Subgroup attempted a very preliminary assessment to identify the kinds of environmental impacts frequently mentioned as environmental justice concerns. To update its sense of the potential and limitations of an approach that selected categories of permits for environmental justice implementation, the Subgroup reflected on what its members have heard over the years as sources of environmental justice concern.

The Subgroup reviewed prior reports and recalled public listening sessions. They compiled an inventory of what was collectively heard from grassroots community groups about the sources of environmental justice concerns. In addition, the NEJAC, informally asked several hundred members of the public who participated in a public conference call held on September 23, 2010, to tell us which activities or permits were of concern; their recommendations were added to the list. The inventory compiled from all of these sources can be found in Appendix B of this report.

Council members have limited knowledge of the details of all of EPA's permitting processes and policies, and even less knowledge of those processes across the country implemented by other federal agencies, tribes and states. However, we made an effort to evaluate the concerns brought to NEJAC's attention over the years by community groups and members of tribal communities. We attempted to link those concerns with permitting programs where EPA has direct authority or oversight over authority delegated to the states. For some concerns (hazardous waste disposal facilities, for example), EPA has authority under several programs to conduct environmental justice reviews and responses. For others, only one statutory authority – or none at all – appeared to provide an avenue to address environmental justice. In order to judge the scope of environmental justice concerns covered by the kinds of permits EPA might decide to select for environmental justice consideration, first it would be helpful to know the total number of facilities and permits issued under each of the statutory programs EPA specified as candidates for their environmental justice in permitting initiative.

This rudimentary inventory was conducted because it was important to do so before giving recommendations. The Subgroup wondered how many sources of environmental justice concern are applicable to permits versus those that are not, and what is the number of permits in each category that would be included in a new environmental justice regulation, policy, guidance, or other EPA action. This is important to understand both administrative feasibility and impact on the ground in terms of making progress in environmental justice communities.

In the initial projection, we found that of the 117 environmental justice concerns listed:

- 21 were addressed under the Clean Air Act,
- 25 were addressed under the Resource Conservation and Recovery Act (RCRA) which governs hazardous waste), although for 17 of the 25 concerns, the specific environmental justice concerns would be addressed only at RCRA facilities and would go unaddressed at sources without a RCRA permit obligation (note: businesses can legally generate hazardous waste without needing a permit),
- 13 were addressed under the Clean Water Act,
- 2 were addressed under the Safe Drinking Water Act,
- 4 were addressed under the Toxic Substances Control Act (TSCA), although half of the specific environmental justice concerns would be addressed only at a TSCA-permitted facility and would go unaddressed at sources without a TSCA permit obligation, and
- 75 or 64 percent would not be addressed by a permit.

This kind of understanding is important. NEJAC has repeatedly said that EPA (and authorized states and tribes) must take a comprehensive, community-based approach to addressing environmental justice. Focusing only on a limited subset of permits can leave communities with concerns based on other activities without a mode of redress.

Recommendations:

2. Maintain an easily accessible "living" document of all permit-related factors that contribute to environmental justice concerns as EPA continues to hear from communities about new issues of concern.
3. Assemble data and inform the public on the percentage of permits that address environmental justice concerns in terms of EPA-issued and EPA-delegated permits, as well as applicable environmental permits. Before proceeding in selecting one or more categories of permits to pursue, EPA should understand and communicate to the public the scope of coverage that will result. This information is important to give communities with environmental justice concerns fair expectations of the attention they are likely to receive. The type of information should include:

    - EPA-issued permits would cover xx% of the activities identified,
    - EPA-delegated permits would cover xx%,
    - RCRA permits would cover xx%; Clean Air Act permits would cover xx%; etc.

3.3   Concerns with the Selection of Permits to Target for Environmental Justice Consideration

Many complexities tie environmental justice and permitting together beyond simply the types of permits. After thinking about what environmental justice concerns might be covered by the various permits, as discussed above, it was clear that there were many questions that EPA would need to consider in selecting the type of permit or even whether selecting categories of permits to pursue first is the best approach. These complexities are related to the charge; but there was not adequate time in the three months allotted to fully discuss each charge question or to interact with EPA staff on these considerations. Such discussion would be appropriate if EPA chooses to convene a longer-term Work

Group. EPA's charge and a compilation of our questions are included in Appendix A, "EPA's Permitting Charge and Council Questions."

Answers to these and other relevant questions would require hearing from EPA staff, particularly from regional offices where EPA and state- and tribal-issued permit dynamics are actually taking place. Likewise, hearing from a sample of delegated or authorized states and tribes would be equally if not more important given the extensive scope of delegation of EPA's permitting authority. Because more agencies than EPA and the delegated states are involved in permitting, further exploration of these delegated permitting activities is warranted. The federal Interagency Working Group on Environmental Justice may need to become involved in this discussion since many permits related to environmental justice concerns are administered by other federal agencies.

Permitting and enforcing permit conditions: The creation of a permit and the enforcement of its conditions are two elements that need to be addressed together. This is particularly relevant to EPA's oversight when enforcement is primarily up to states (or others under EPA's oversight). Review and enforcement may or may not take place in an equitable manner.

Recommendations.

4. <u>Provide compliance assistance by EPA, states, and tribes to ensure permit conditions are met.</u> Compliance histories need to be reviewed and taken into account when permit applications to renew or expand existing facilities are under evaluation. EPA can use these permit applications to obtain better compliance monitoring and negotiate pollution reductions in some instances.

5. <u>Learn from positive examples.</u> As EPA addresses the questions needed to incorporate environmental justice into permitting, it would be important to learn from positive examples. NEJAC on many occasions, for example, has cited the effectiveness of EPA's Community Action for a Renewed Environment (CARE) program. That program may well have examples where environmental justice was successfully incorporated into facility permits to the benefit of the affected community.

    *   *Tribal perspective:* The Council heard that EPA has improved its advance notification to tribes of permit activity. This is welcomed, and we encourage the Agency to do even more (and earlier) coordination of this nature.
    *   *State perspective:* From a state perspective, we have learned that incorporating environmental justice early in the permitting process reduces the time it takes to review and issue a permit. The public should be made aware of prospective permit applications prior to the state's reaching the technical sufficiency stage of permit review, and before the legal notice of application is published. Permit conditions that satisfy all parties should be incorporated before the formal public comment period is announced. Early, meaningful public involvement prior to reaching tentative determination eliminates the need for costly and time-consuming formal adjudicatory hearings. For example, the State of Connecticut requires that applicants in environmental justice communities draft a public outreach plan detailing efforts to be taken. Those efforts include a mandatory informational public meeting coordinated with approval and oversight by the Environmental Justice Program office. The public participation plan required is in the form of a template that is provided to applicants to guide them through the process and provide the state with relevant information for evaluation.[1]

---

[1] The Connecticut public participation template can be viewed at: www.ct.gov/dep/environmentaljustice.

6. <u>Support TSCA reform to better identify the range and toxicity characteristics of current chemicals in use, and their applicability to permitted pollution in communities (and elsewhere).</u> Permits involving the use and/or discharge of chemicals need to specifically declare *all* chemicals that may be discharged. Information about the use of toxic chemicals, to ensure that risks relative to their use can be understood, will help affirm that such uses are appropriate. This is a fundamental Community Right-to-Know issue in direct support of better assessment of cumulative risks and protecting all communities. Our nation's out-of-date chemical policy under the TSCA needs to incorporate this concept. A similar process already is in play in Europe through REACH – the Registration, Evaluation, Authorization and Restriction of Chemical Substances Act.[2] That new law entered into force on 1 June 2007 and serves as a real model for EPA and this country on chemical use policy revision and development.

4.0   ANSWERS TO EPA'S SPECIFIC CHARGE QUESTIONS

4.1   Question 1 – Types of Permits Issued by EPA: *"What types of EPA permits should [EPA] be looking at now, to work to incorporate environmental justice concerns into EPA's permits?"*

Over the course of its 16-year life span, NEJAC has repeatedly asked EPA to incorporate environmental justice into its permitting processes, and has provided specific advice as to how it should be done. For example, in 1999, NEJAC's Waste and Facility Siting Subcommittee worked with EPA's Office of Solid Waste and Emergency Response to develop EPA guidance, "Social Aspects of Siting RCRA Hazardous Waste Facilities."[3] That document set out a checklist that permit writers would use to identify all relevant community concerns and conditions, conduct enhanced community outreach and communication, provide community members with the technical background needed for meaningful dialogue, and encourage discussions that would take all relevant community concerns into account.

Similarly, in 2000, NEJAC's "Regulatory Strategy for Siting and Operating Waste Transfer Stations"[4], recommended that EPA create guidance that would take environmental justice into consideration in siting, substantive design and operating conditions, and public participation, referring to other NEJAC work products: "NEJAC Public Participation Model" and "Environmental Justice, Urban Revitalization, and Brownfields: The Search for Authentic Signs of Hope."

More recent reports have shifted focus from kinds of permits in which EPA should incorporate environmental justice in specified ways, to looking at communities where all permits and other activities of environmental justice concern should be evaluated and routes to improve environmental justice pursued. The shift from a focus on a particular permit to a more holistic, area-wide approach specifically was addressed in NEJAC's 2004 report, "Ensuring Risk Reduction in Communities with Multiple Stressors: Environmental Justice and Cumulative Risks/Impacts.[5]" In that report, the concept of proportionality was clearly laid out:[6]

> *"The concept of proportional response is a direct outgrowth of the NEJAC's thinking about*

---

[2] See http://ec.europa.eu/environment/chemicals/reach/reach_intro.htm
[3] See http://www.epa.gov/osw/hazard/tsd/permit/site/k00005.pdf.
[4] See http://www.epa.gov/compliance/environmentaljustice/resources/publications/nejac/waste-trans-reg-strtgy.pdf
[5] See http://www.epa.gov/compliance/environmentaljustice/resources/publications/nejac/nejac-cum-risk-rpt-122104
[6] NEJAC Cumulative Risk Report, pages 32 and 33

conducting cumulative risk analysis in the context of a bias for action and its promotion of a collaborative problem-solving model for addressing cumulative risks and impacts. The idea of proportional response seeks to match the needs of communities and tribes with an appropriate level or type of analysis and action at any given point. In other words, analysis should be commensurate with community needs and the nature of the intervention to be taken. Figure 6, above, attempts to capture the idea of proportional response. Response also must be proportional to the harm caused. In nearly all communities with environmental justice issues, the adverse effect results from environmental impacts from multiple sources, some large and some small. The key to engaging the sources of impact in collaborative problem-solving and achieving meaningful pollution reduction in the short- and long-term is the expectation of proportional responsibility on the part of all contributors to the harm. Those with the most severe impacts should be held to the most aggressive and significant response. Those with lesser impacts should be expected to contribute their fair share to community improvement. This proportional approach is the most likely to engender immediate, positive response because the causation is clear and the expectation of pollution reduction sensible and achievable.

"This proportional response can be contrasted with the "tipping point" approach where a facility needing a permit in an overburdened area becomes the sole target for pollution prevention. Simply because a facility's permit is due for renewal or the facility is seeking siting or expansion, it becomes the enforcement target on the grounds that this new or renewed pollution is the "straw that breaks the camel's back." This kind of approach has many downsides, however. Where the stakes are so high–attainment of a permit to operate–the level of legal and political resistance escalates. Facility lawyers seek every means to avoid facility closure by construing regulatory authority narrowly. Efforts by the facility manager to work with the community to address concerns and recognize community needs take a back seat to litigation over "requirements." Regulators charged with addressing the issues become vulnerable to politicians bemoaning the threat to jobs. Moreover, the other sources of pollution in the area rest easy, confident that they have no responsibility for their own emissions and that the permitted facility will bear the brunt of controversy and attention. The result can impact needed economic development, and it wholly misses the opportunity to engage each contributor of a community burden in the process of making the community whole and healthy. The proportional approach, in contrast, seeks to identify relative impacts using screening tools, to confront each source of environmental burden with a rough sense of its accountability, to educate the polluting sources about community needs and vulnerabilities, and to build working relationships that lead to overall pollution reduction. Creative alliances can emerge where a large source of emissions can team with smaller sources to cost-effectively reduce the community's burden. These discussions are particularly fruitful where community driven, so that the community members can identify the issues of highest concern and provide insight into ways the polluting sources can reduce their impacts. These dialogues are the best way to appreciate and respond in a holistic way to the aggregation of stressors in a community.

"It is important to recognize, however, that not all contributors will be willing to come to the table. Some sources may resist a collaborative problem-solving process, preferring to lie in the weeds and expect other businesses to take care of the problem. Some may continue to narrowly construe their regulatory obligations to protect human health. Some may go further, actively causing environmental deterioration by violating even the terms of their own permits. In some cases, the polluting party is an arm or agent of federal, state or local government, and intergovernmental relations strain the regulatory authority's ability to mandate strict enforcement of environmental controls. In these circumstances, the proportional approach again provides a direction: Those who do not accept their proportional degree of accountability should be subject to a proportional degree of extra enforcement to coerce accountability and pollution prevention where it cannot be

> *encouraged by other means.*
> "*In both views of the proportional response, the linchpin is community involvement and multi-stakeholder consensus building. There is no "one size fits all" remedy, but instead the approach must be a search for all applicable legal authorities, an engagement with the community to understand and seek direction on the means to reduce cumulative impacts, and an on-going expectation that all sources of environmental burden will contribute their share to its reduction or elimination.*"

The approach recommended in NEJAC's cumulative risk report became the foundation for EPA's CARE program, which NEJAC in 2010 and prior years recommended be expanded. The approach is made workable by employing tools like EPA's Environmental Justice Strategic Enforcement Screening Tool (EJ SEAT), which NEJAC evaluated in 2009, and facilitated by EPA's EJView Mapping Tool.[7]

We summarize these key prior NEJAC documents here because they are directly relevant to EPA's 2010 request that we identify the kinds of permits in which the Agency should begin to incorporate environmental justice. Previous Councils have considered in great detail the way environmental justice should be considered in permits and the limits to what can be accomplished by an ad hoc permit approach.

Reflecting on the geographic rather than single permit approach, the NEJAC again notes that a cumulative impact approach will substantially help assure that environmental justice concerns can be addressed across all media. Many facilities have multiple permits (often issued by multiple agencies), and most environmental justice communities have concerns with multiple facilities and impacts across multiple media. If EPA proceeds on a permit category by permit category approach, it may develop different standards under different programs. It should not be easier to "pass" the environmental justice test for an air permit versus a water discharge permit, etc., when both impact the same location.

Recommendation:

7. <u>Follow the consensus recommendations of relevant prior NEJAC reports.</u> The NEJAC also recognizes that in the intervening period, EPA's practices and community needs may have changed. A current review by EPA of permitting and environmental justice gaps would be helpful to this discussion. What has EPA addressed in the years after previous NEJAC reports were delivered to the EPA Administrator? Has recent experience suggested that NEJAC should re-consider its advice in light of changed circumstances, or does the consensus of these previous reports continue to provide a fundamental answer to EPA's questions?

   - Environmental justice and robust public participation should be part of every permit [8]
   - Authorities under every permitting program are available and should be employed to seek environmental justice [9]
   - Environmental justice concerns arise in a geographic area, not just within the bounds of a particular permit, and EPA should focus on locating and improving places with high cumulative

---

[7]   See NEJAC, Nationally Consistent Screening Approaches, http://www.epa.gov/compliance/ej/resources/publications/nejac/ej-screening-approaches-rpt-2010.pdf and http://epamap14.epa.gov/ejmap/entry.html.
[8]   See http://www.epa.gov/compliance/ej/resources/publications/nejac/permit-recom-report-0700.pdf
[9]   See http://www.epa.gov/compliance/ej/resources/publications/nejac/permit-recom-report-0700.pdf

risks and impacts rather than rely on a permit-by-permit approach.[10] There are tools available to screen for locations of high environmental justice concern.[11]

8. Increase and maintain active listening, engagement, and follow-up with communities. Community meetings sponsored by EPA provide meaningful opportunities for community engagement, exchange of ideas, networking and historical context and background. EPA, states, and tribes have to make these opportunities more regular and easily accessible to all. Such local meetings have included the following permit-related suggestions worthy of EPA, state, and tribal considerations:

- Permit conditions should recognize and address at least one or a few environmental justice community-initiated and environmentally-related priorities. Build an appropriate mechanism into permitting to support this.
- Develop proposals to better address and protect indigenous peoples' cultural and subsistence resources through permitting.
- Negotiate permits and Supplemental Environmental Projects (SEPs) to include more or enhanced local environmental monitoring, timely public releases of facility-specific data, and supported, open analysis of the data relative to the host community's environmental justice priorities and concerns.
- Help communities develop and adopt community-specific, comprehensive, environmental justice plans before new or renewed/modified permits are considered – as much as practicable. This may be one of the strongest mechanisms to allow for cumulative-impact assessment and provide for local community engagement in the process. Such a local environmental justice plan would establish a community-based baseline against which all current and future permits are gauged for environmental and public health impact. All permitted or otherwise legal environmental activities would be measured against such a plan. If EPA and states/tribes need a comprehensive, long-range environmental justice Plan, surely communities do too.

Community groups have emphasized the importance of effective enforcement of Title VI of the Civil Rights Act and reminded EPA of the need for final guidance to the states. Title VI compliance is an important element of environmental justice in permitting.

Pursuing environmental justice in the public participation process. Previous NEJAC reports have been valuable in setting out ways to engage the public in permitting proceedings (and other efforts to pursue environmental justice in an environmentally overburdened community). Advice on public engagement by the NEJAC remains pertinent today.[12]

Also of note is Chapter 40 Code of Federal Regulations (CFR) § 124, "Procedures for Decisionmaking," the rule that describes how multiple environmental laws and permits are to be processed. Specifically, "Subpart A," the first part of this law, describes the steps EPA will follow in receiving permit applications, preparing draft permits, issuing public notices, inviting public comment and holding public hearings on draft permits. Subpart A also covers assembling an administrative record, responding to comments, issuing a final permit decision, and allowing for administrative appeal of final permit decisions." (§ 124.1, Purpose and scope (b)). This law specifically applies to the Clean Water Act (although it is not applicable to the Army Corps of Engineers), the Safe Drinking Water Act, and RCRA. The Act is applicable to delegated states and tribes (124.1 subpart (e)). This law ". . . allows [permit] applications to be jointly

---

[10] See http://www.epa.gov/compliance/ej/resources/publications/nejac/nejac-cum-risk-rpt-122104.pdf
[11] See http://www.epa.gov/compliance/ej/resources/publications/nejac/ej-screening-approaches-rpt-2010.pdf)
[12] See: http://www.epa.gov/compliance/ej/resources/publications/nejac/model-public-part-plan.pdf.

processed, joint comment periods and hearings to be held, and final permits to be issued on a cooperative basis <u>whenever EPA and a State agree to take such steps</u> in general or in individual cases. These joint processing agreements may be provided in the <u>Memoranda of Agreement</u> ..." (subpart (f), underline emphasis added). Agreements of this nature, including Memoranda of Agreement, are addressed later in this report. This provision includes the procedures to be taken to ensure sufficient public participation in permitting under a number of EPA programs.

<u>Recommendations:</u>

9. <u>Fully exercise and leverage this overarching regulation to maximize public engagement in all permitting processes, regardless of type.</u>

10. <u>Review, through regional and HQ permit-process and implementation staff and leaders, the numerous documents that provide guidance about permitting, and immediately begin to focus on incorporating their principles into all possible agreements, formal or otherwise, with delegated states and other federal permitting entities.</u>

11. <u>Draft an Outreach Plan template, or form, for use by EPA permit staff.</u> The plan would contain all relevant community concerns and conditions as identified in the "state perspective" bullet under the discussion of "Learning from positive examples." This plan would facilitate the permit applicant's ability to perform meaningful public involvement. The information requested in the plan would serve to guide the applicant through an outreach or communication process. The plan should include a list of stakeholders, focused on known tribal nations, environmental justice communities, and other indigenous peoples.

12. <u>Maintain, in its regional offices, an open list of community organizations and tribal government and indigenous organization contacts.</u> This resource list should be provided directly to permit applicants. The applicant's plan would be reviewed and approved before a public informational meeting occurs to ensure all relevant stakeholders are contacted with proper advanced notice. EPA staff should attend the public meetings to ascertain whether additional meetings need to occur to clarify the proposed project and to ascertain whether a facilitator is needed to enable productive dialogue. In this process, EPA and the public would have a ready-made document available from the prospective permit applicant to describe prospective project activities to be taken by the applicant within or near the impacted community. EPA could require this document as part of the permit's technical sufficiency review. This can provide the community and the applicant the ability to clear up questions and misunderstandings regarding the proposed project and avoid a long and costly formal adjudicatory hearing.

    A pre-application meeting with prospective applicants also should be encouraged by EPA permit writers to discuss environmental justice and tribal considerations pertinent and related to the permit. This meeting would provide a good opportunity to discuss the outreach efforts the applicant would be required to undertake as part of the public notice requirement. The templates could then be shared with states, enabling better guidance and a streamlining of the public participation process. EPA regional offices would provide training to the states. A sample template that has proven to work well for state governments can be found at http://www.ct.gov/dep/lib/dep/environmental_justice/EJ_Plan.pdf

Supplemental Environmental Projects (SEP). SEP "projects" are negotiated between EPA, the authorized state or tribal program, and the regulated entity or business when enforcement penalties are being settled against a facility that has been in violation of a permit or environmental law. SEPs are different from permit modifications in that SEPs are triggered by enforcement settlement negotiations, whereas, permit modifications are 'applied for' by a facility when its conditions change relative to its current permit (typically not related to enforcement). Permit modifications, as implemented through established procedures, DO allow for direct public tracking and engagement; SEPs do not. Although SEPs can occur when a rule or permit condition has been violated, EPA should evaluate whether the SEP concept has broader applicability in the permitting process relative to environmental justice. Why should a SEP require a violation?

The concept of the SEP is to allow a partial reduction in the penalty fee if the violating facility willingly redirects that partial reduction into a 'supplemental environmental project.' Typically, SEPs are invested back into the community near the facility at fault, ideally to further mitigate problems or risks associated with the facility, or to otherwise invest in an appropriate (environmental protection-based) project to enhance the community. The purchase of a 'Haz-Mat' emergency response truck, or an investment in a neighborhood stream enhancement project are examples. Required clean-ups and costs associated with getting back into compliance are not eligible for SEPs. The dollar value of a proposed SEP cannot substantially reduce the potential "full" cost of the penalty; the SEP should not diminish the penalty's impact as an incentive for the violator to stay in compliance.

Importantly, SEPs are optional for the penalized facility; neither EPA, a state, nor any other interested party can require such projects in the penalty phase -- the owner of the penalized facility has to want to do it. The question then is, what can be done to encourage SEPs more frequently? EPA, states, and tribes do not have to passively wait for such an offer. They know well in advance when enforcement efforts are underway. They can plan for, research, and lay appropriate environmental justice-oriented groundwork for SEP options during this time. Is this happening? If not, why not?

Environmental law enforcement is complicated, time and resource intensive, and, understandably, is carried out in a careful and confidential manner. It can easily take years for a given penalty to be issued and settled after appeals. It is often a long drawn-out process before SEPs are even considered during the final settlement phase of a penalty case. In part because of the long time frame, NEJAC believes more can be done to tie environmental justice community needs to the SEP process. For example, once an enforcement case is settled but before the final penalty is negotiated, the Regional EPA office could prepare SEP suggestions based on prior and currently active engagement with the hosting environmental justice community.

Recommendations:

13. Elevate the use of SEPs to a much higher and more open priority by EPA and the states. If the penalized facilities can't be forced to negotiate SEPs, what can be done to entice them? Specifically, what can EPA regions and delegated states or tribes do to "prime this pump" and be ready to foster environmental justice-enhancing SEPs? Since communities are excluded from such negotiations, EPA, states, and tribes have to be ready to work on the communities' behalf to help this tool be proactively considered and used as intended. This is not a conflict of interest for EPA, states, or tribes; they can (and should) ensure enforcement and penalties and assertively negotiate for the good of the facilities' host community through SEPs.

14. Encourage greater use of SEPs by developing, hosting, and publicizing training and implementation sessions for how the Agency includes environmental justice-oriented, pro-active SEP options in all

penalty settlement efforts. EPA can specify the same from the authorized states/tribes through the agreements, noted further in this report (Agreements with States and Tribes). The training and implementation should include clear advice and tools to help a penalized facility that *wants* to invest in its host community – beyond the enticement of a slight cost reduction. Clearly, SEPs directly offer more to the host community as well as the facility itself and the state or tribe by keeping some of the penalty monies from going into the national coffers. EPA and states should do everything possible to help this happen. Additonally, SEP investments can only improve the facilities' ties to community leaders and neighbors. Use of this tool to help mend adversarial relationships between the facilities and their host communities (and with the regulatory role of the penalizing agency) is a fundamental part of regulatory and permitting enforcement. It should be noted that investing in host communities via SEPs is not an attempt to buy host community silence, but rather an attempt to demonstrate remorse over the violation having occurred as well as improving the local environment.

Employing Environmental Justice/"Good Neighbor"/Environmental Benefit Agreements as part of permitting

Permit negotiations, if handled well, are an opportunity to evaluate and provide tangible measures to better balance or reverse the trends of disproportionate impact – beyond minimum requirements. One way of doing so is through the negotiations of environmental benefit agreements during the permitting process. The negotiation process has considerable flexibility and can include agreements on emission reductions at existing facilities and cleanup of contaminated property. These agreements could even extend to such benefits as funding for improving the indoor air quality at local schools, etc. A permit applicant may likely welcome community participation in these negotiations if it means that they will avoid a long, costly adjudicatory hearing that may jeopardize the project or the applicant's standing in the region. These agreements also can be effectively used by states mandated by their legislatures to reduce the permitting review times and operate in a business-friendly manner.

Good neighbor agreements provide the community a direct way to negotiate for tangible benefits like the use of cleaner fuels, the best pollution control equipment available, enhanced local monitoring and reporting, or for a project that can remediate an existing pollution burden. Since this is supplemental to the formal permitting process, it does not have to be negotiated by the primacy agency, yet it could still be referenced within a permit. This is where EPA and/or the primacy agency can help: bring the community and the permit-related facility representatives together to consider this option. Presuming parties are willing, such agreements can be directly negotiated between the facility and 'the community' – however that may be defined. This kind of agreement has broader potential than the SEP concept described above because there is more flexibility and the opportunity for direct communication among the parties without the legal constraints that are part of the SEP process.

Recommendation:

15. Help communities employ environmental justice/"Good Neighbor"/Environmental Benefit Agreements as part of permitting in order to more proactively resolve environmental justice concerns. EPA should consider a more proactive approach to resolving environmental justice concerns as part of permitting.

Understanding Tribal and Indigenous communities and permitting. There are too many special considerations related to tribal and indigenous peoples and permitting to be responsibly addressed in this report. Although we had active participation of our tribal representatives, additional perspectives are needed to fully inform recommendations. The NEJAC feels it must again highlight the critical, ongoing need for EPA and all permitting entities to pay particular attention to the many unique environmental justice challenges that exacerbate adverse impacts on native populations, whether they're in the Midwest, Guam, Alaska or Puerto Rico. Examples of these complexities include:

- Federal (let alone state) recognition of tribes, bands, and confederated nations – whatever the structure – is not uniformly recognized by permitting agencies.
- Some federally-recognized tribes are not recognized by the respective state(s).
- Some state-recognized tribes are not federally recognized.
- Jurisdictions surrounding these dynamics and permitting becomes very complicated and a greater barrier to realizing environmental justice.
- Permit (and other) litigation between tribes and EPA and/or other permitting entities is counter-productive and expensive, often beyond the means of tribes and their communities.
- Often, tribal/indigenous-related environmental justice challenges are in our nation's most remote, under served, cost-prohibitive places to reach, let alone cleanup and protect.
- There can be up to 13 federal agencies with some authority over tribal land management, permitting, enforcement, etc. Yet they often do not talk with each other; thus coordination, especially with the tribes, is lost. This is a particular opportunity for the newly revitalized Interagency Working Group for Environmental Justice.

Recommendation:

16. Given the severity of these environmental justice barriers and the need for specific attention and resources to properly address them, EPA should do more to ensure ample representation from both tribal leaders and tribal communities appointed to the Council and related work groups. This is not about proportionate representation; rather, it is about going beyond minimal representation to ensure adequate and well-supported participation by these interests.

Avoidance of Emergency Permits: Despite the urgency of response needed during the recent (summer of 2010) Deepwater Horizon oil spill off the Louisiana coast, EPA informed the Council that exemptions from current permitting requirements were neither sought nor granted by EPA. This is the right approach. Advanced planning for emergencies and applying lessons learned from past incidents demonstrates that critical environmental protections can work even during emergencies. Permitting involves many variables and potential long-term complications that require careful, deliberative considerations by all potentially impacted populations.

Recommendation:

17. Avoid emergency permits. The Council advises EPA that it would be a good practice to NOT issue emergency permits. Although the Council understands and respects that emergencies often require regulatory flexibility, nonetheless, emergency permitting should be avoided whenever possible.

Recent Additional Input on Types of Permits to be Included in EPA's Environmental Justice in Permitting Strategy. In the public conference call discussion of this NEJAC charge in September 2010, the following activities were noted as topics of particular interest to this charge:

- Clean Water Act and Underground Injection Controls (UIC) -- Are these programs adequate?

- Federal Insecticide, Fungicide, Rodenticide Act (FIFRA) – Pesticides have long been a critical concern for environmental justice communities. It may be good to bring more EPA/outreach to environmental justice communities dealing with pesticides, as well as farm worker groups and public health advocates working in this arena.

Care in continually reviewing pesticide registrations is important, but it also is important for EPA (and sister federal agencies – via the Environmental Justice Interagency Working Group) to enhance protection of those living and working in areas affected by pesticide drift, contamination of soil and groundwater, and ingestion of pesticides near application areas. In addition, communities have raised serious concerns about enforcement of the rodenticide application requirements of this act, particularly where children are poisoned by compounds distributed in forms that make exposure more likely.

Certainly, due to the high numbers of non-English speaking and/or reading workers, family members and neighboring residents, reliance on proper use and precautions based on posting directions and warnings is entirely ineffective within these populations. Exposure is common; viable solutions are needed.

- Air permits -- Although States likely issue more of these permits than does EPA, EPA still maintains key, unique roles within air permitting. One is a need to provide clarifying guidance on the integration of environmental justice and cumulative risk concerns into the air pollution emissions permitting process. This is also appropriate for the second question of the charge, addressed later in this report.

- Concentrated Animal Feeding Operations (CAFO) – NEJAC continues to hear regularly of concerns about inadequate environmental justice surrounding this issue. It appears that EPA maintains a significant role here under the Clean Water Act in terms of possible groundwater contamination, and significant water body deterioration from CAFO runoff, Total Maximum Daily Load limits, etc. Odor and air emissions from these facilities may also tie to permitting issues in need of more environmental justice attention.

Advice Specific to EPA's Focus per Relevant Permit 'Type'. Acknowledging the proceeding caveats, the following overview is considered a good start for enhanced environmental justice focus by EPA's leadership and permitting programs. In making these program-specific comments, the NEJAC realizes that these types of permits are not always in EPA's direct control. However, we believe that to a large, if not always complete extent, EPA is either in direct control of the permitting process or has direct oversight capabilities and obligations, regardless of primacy. This list of permit types has been brought to the Council's attention through NEJAC public conference calls, individual Council members, review of prior NEJAC documents, Subgroup research and expertise, and Subgroup discussions with EPA staff.

Clean Air Act. Clean Air Act permits set guidelines and carryout provisions for *considerations for alternative sites.* This is connected to EPA's "New Source Review" (NSR) and the "Prevention of Significant Deterioration" (PSD) permitting activities.

Recommendation:

18. Review *Clean Air Act* permits for incorporation of environmental justice. When reviewing Clean Air Act permits for incorporation of environmental justice, EPA should be mindful of the following:

- How often is environmental justice currently considered in these permits, and how often are alternative sites evaluated? Is this is really done?
- If this analysis is considered, is it meaningful? Can it be? How?
- Delegated states need more guidance on the process and a mechanism to be held accountable by EPA so that this does happen where appropriate.
- EPA needs to exercise this agency discretionary tool. It was put there for a purpose; don't let it be lost because of atrophy. The Subgroup believes the intent of this provision is good, so use it with intentionality and clarity. The law says, "consider." Clarify what this really means. Make it an overt, pro-active, community-oriented (however defined) consideration, with the engagement of the applicants and multiple regulatory entities.
- Build clear cumulative impact considerations into the NSR process.
- Currently, the notion of such a consideration seems to be in a quagmire, helping no one, likely costing EPA and others money, and providing the basis for legal challenges from the regulated community. There are raised expectations by the public that have been undermined by a bad process. How can the process be re-imagined to make environmental justice a uniform, organized part of the decision-making process?

Clean Water Act - §"404" permits regarding the 'Discharge of Dredge or Fill Material: In the case of surface coal mining, EPA has concerns with §404 and §402. The Council believes these permits can achieve important environmental justice goals:

- These permits, particularly tied to Mountain Top Removal (MTR) mining and stream protections, have come to the Council's attention as mechanisms that need clarification and stronger enforcement.
- In relation to MTR mining, often permits for this type of activity impact very rural, small and isolated communities. This exacerbates local environmental burdens and inhibits communication to states and larger communities of downstream impacts.
- There are multiple permitting conditions that hamper communication between all relevant parties. In addition to U.S. Army Corps of Engineers (USACE) §404 permits, states will typically issue the related §402 water discharge permits (NPDES) and the federal Surface Mining and Reclamation Control Act permits. In general, coordination and communication across these bureaucracies related to environmental justice concerns appears to be less than optimal; some have suggested it's nonexistent.
- Between the initial public review/input opportunity related to a §404 permit application and the final permit, a year may pass. During this time, permit details may dramatically change from what was initially proposed. The next public opportunity to learn of permit modifications is when the permit is in final form, and therefore too late for the public, EPA or the host states to be able to modify or mitigate for environmental justice concerns. This is a dysfunctional process that needs senior-level attention by EPA, USACE, and possibly the Interagency Working Group.
- National Environmental Policy Act (NEPA) reviews and the scope of Environmental Impact Statements (EIS) are carried out by the USACE. There is a consistent view (based on specific local experiences) that the USACE does not look at the broad scope of potential local environmental impacts of a project or permit activity (if not specifically required by NEPA) including impacts on human health and the environment.
- EPA/USACE coordinated engagement and EPA's oversight need dramatic improvement in this area. Fundamentally, EPA is in charge of the Clean Water Act, and thus (one may infer) 40 C.F.R. 124 – public participation processes are just as applicable to the USACE. Where is EPA's accountability to address problems related to the USACE's limited public participation procedures?

- Enforcement. What if the USACE doesn't enforce the permit's conditions? Can EPA take over or somehow require the USACE to step up? What is the case record of USACE's enforcement and penalties related to §404 permits?

Recommendations:

19. Incorporate a closer and/or independent review of the formal consideration of environmental justice concerns by the USACE, EPA, tribes, states and local jurisdictions regarding not only the issuance and enforcement of Clean Water Act §402 permits (issued by states or other delegated authorities) and §404 permits on Discharge of Dredge or Fill Material (issued by USACE). Perhaps the greatest need here is for more information sharing, particularly from USACE, which EPA has had little influence over. This clearly suggests an opportunity for the Interagency Working Group to help the USACE do more than the minimal requirements within their own rules and procedures.

20. Facilitate better coordination between the various permitting entities issuing permits for MTR mining activities and projects. EPA should seek a balance between state efforts to "streamline" permitting of these types of activities, and greater engagement of affected communities in the permitting process for surface mining. Residents of affected communities have requested via the NEJAC that EPA establish that Community Right-to-Know and public engagement, as well as protecting public health and ecological resources, have primacy when juxtaposed against MTR permit applications.

21. Re-affirm the necessity of undertaking Environmental Impact Assessments and/or Environmental Reviews of all MTR-proposed projects, especially those that propose to move massive amounts of land as required under NEPA. Such reviews also increase the opportunities for public review, comment, engagement, and appropriate modification for amendment or repeal of final permits. This is needed urgently.

Hydraulic Fracturing (or Fracking): This activity is covered (with ambiguity) within 'Underground Injection Controls' (UICs) of the Safe Drinking Water Act. It is also tied to the Clean Water Act. The 2005 Energy Policy Act excluded hydraulic fracturing from regulation under the Safe Drinking Water Act, but communities have made clear that current permitting obligations are inadequate.

- When recovered fracking fluids (flowback) are discharged to a surface source, the regulation of these fluids fall within a NPDES permit under the Clean Water Act. In addition, if the flowback is disposed through reinjection back into underground aquifers, this action is regulated through the Underground Injection Control program of the Safe Water Drinking Act as a Class II reinjection well.

- Because the action of hydraulic fracturing is not regulated, there is **non**-transparency in environmental impact reviews (e.g., National Environmental Policy Act review), leading up to the development of new energy resources. Unless the public is aware that fracking will be part of the process in natural gas/oil development, public comments and concerns do not become part of the permitting public record. On this point, it's important to also note that the U.S. Department of Interior is currently looking to streamline permitting processes that allow for fracking so that the development of "cleaner" natural gas can occur faster, in keeping with an increased demand of natural gas versus coal energy. This is another example where EPA needs to work aggressively to provide better and more consistent environmental protections across federal agencies.

- There's a fundamental environmental justice and Community Right-to-Know problem with whatever permitting may be tied to this process. Un-named chemicals, protected as "proprietary information," are pumped into the ground to assist in well drilling operations. These chemicals can potentially contaminate surface and ground water that at times is also the source of drinking water in rural communities.

Recommendations:

22. Include the full disclosure of the chemicals used and an assurance that such use is appropriate and safe. Residual contamination as a result of the fracking process should not be allowed. This type of information sharing would be entirely consistent with the federal Emergency Planning and Community Right-to-Know Act (EPCRA), and could be implemented in a similar fashion, perhaps even incorporated into the EPCRA laws.

23. Work with states to initially develop more protective standards and policies surrounding hydraulic fracturing. EPA has limited regulatory authority to permit this activity based on congressionally imposed limitations. EPA also should develop proposals to expand EPA, state, and tribal protective permitting options, rules, and statutes related to hydraulic fracturing and the chemicals used in the process.

RCRA Hazardous Waste Permits, Section 3005c(3): This omnibus section of the law requires that RCRA permits contain all conditions necessary to protect human health and the environment. To the extent this section *is applied to both* the permitting *process and its enforcement* once the permit has been issued, this subject likely deserves more attention by EPA.

• In the 1995 case, *In re Chemical Waste Management of Indiana, Inc.*, the EPA Appeals Board ruled that "Each permit issued under this section shall contain such terms and conditions as the Administrator (or the State) determines necessary to protect human health and the environment." In the eyes of community groups, this means that unless the facility in question has zero emissions, can their permit be supported and/or approved if its incremental releases can<u>not</u> be shown to further protect human health and the environment.

Recommendation:

24. Address the extent to which RCRA §305 is applied to both the permitting process and its enforcement once the permit has been issued. EPA should deal with how this section is addressed when the permitted facility (or one in application for a new permit/renewal/modification) is located in an area already heavily burdened with pollution

4.2. Question 2 – Types Of Permits Delegated To States, Tribes, And Others: *"What types of permits issued pursuant to federal environmental laws, whether they are federal, state, or tribal permits, are best suited for exploring and addressing the complex issue of cumulative impacts from exposure to multiple sources and existing conditions that are critical to the effective consideration of environmental justice in permitting?"*

This question reflects a fundamental conflict. Permits, almost by definition address one facility at a time; cumulative impacts by definition reflect multiple sources of pollution (at least in the context of EPA's authority – there are many other impacts beyond EPA's direct influence, such as reduced access to health care, for example). Again, the NEJAC refers EPA to pertinent recommendations of prior NEJAC councils, cited above in response to Question 1. Indeed, prior NEJAC Councils repeatedly recommended a geographic, rather than permit-by-permit, approach precisely because environmental justice concerns arise in communities overburdened by multiple stressors, and a multi-faceted response is therefore necessary.

The following points are initial responses to EPA; by no mean should they be considered complete. This is another reason the NEJAC recommends that more time and attention be applied to the many facets surrounding environmental justice and cumulative impacts in relation to permitting, regardless of which governmental entity has primacy.

Agreements with States and Tribes: The coordination between EPA's regional offices and the authorized state and tribal programs provides key opportunities for addressing and tracking environmental justice through permitting that are underutilized. That relationship includes regularly renewed formal agreements, some of which provide for public review and engagement. Two types of agreements are the focus of this recommendation: *Performance Partnership Agreements* and *Memoranda of Understanding*.

The Performance Partnership Agreements (PPA) are used by EPA regions and their respective states (and possibly tribes) to spell out how EPA-delegated or authorized work will be carried out. States are accountable for the work they implement under EPA's authority, and they're accountable for the funds they receive to do the work. Although not established in rule or law, the PPAs have been in use for at least the past 10 to 15 years. Because they are not specified in rules/statutes, they are flexible. The agreements can address specific activities under the respective federal laws, as well as address broader common environmental issues of concern including environmental justice, climate change/adaptation, sustainability, and even cumulative impacts. They could also be ignored if the states and EPA don't support them, which the NEJAC believes should not be allowed to happen.

Each state will have its own agreement with EPA. It is typically renewed every two years. When drafted for a new two-year cycle, there should be a public review/comment period of at least 30 days. Notice of this public comment period should be accomplished through press releases, written notice to known environmental justice community leaders and organizations, and made accessible through a dedicated public notification web page on the respective Regional EPA website. After that, the state and EPA should consider and respond to the comments before the PPA is finalized and signed (by the EPA Regional Administrator and the state environmental agency's director).

The State of Washington's practice on public notice of PPAs represents a good model. Washington publishes a draft PPA for a 30-day public comment period. It then takes an additional ~20 days to address each comment in writing. All comments are considered for incorporation into the final PPA, and responses are included in the final PPAs appendix. This is a relatively short and efficient process. Other states may also have good practices including ways to continually update environmental justice contact lists to foster open and regular communication. The NEJAC believes this would be a fruitful area for further EPA inquiry.

Recommendations:

25. NEJAC recommends *both* EPA and the states/tribes be more active and "vocal" in publicizing and enticing multiple stakeholder involvement and public participation with PPAs. Do more to engage the public and tribal communities in the review and renewal of Performance Partnership Agreements. In those cases where tribal communities are not part of given PPAs, EPA should seriously consider offering these opportunities for negotiation to them. This would help to create a stronger and better-aligned relationship through an agreement so the tribes can have the opportunity to communicate their specific needs and EPA could obtain guidance from the tribes on how to improve relations.
26. Require specific language describing what both EPA regional offices and the state/tribe are going to do during the agreement to protect and advance environmental justice. Because the PPA is not legally required, EPA can implement this right away and it would entail relatively low cost to do so. Insert a clear reminder within PPAs that the agreements are tied to the use of federally funds, which includes full adherence to Title VI of the Civil Rights Act.
27. Require PPA language to include a mutual commitment to provide an annual update on the environmental justice elements (and all others) within the agreement, so the public can track progress and know of updates. This too would require relatively low cost.
28. Use the environmental justice elements within the PPA to advance local and regional measures for environmental justice progress. These measures are very hard to define; EPA regional offices, states, tribal nations and communities would need to work through this process together. The PPA can help by triggering regular, publically advertized, commitments to support the environmental justice progress of EPA regions, states, and tribes.
29. Provide a national compendium of commitments and progress updates of regional, state, and tribal PPAs. Post them on the Regional EPA office website specifically dedicated to active ongoing engagement with environmental justice communities in the Regions. Publicize the successes on the website. Let everyone see the good ones; let the good ones be marketing examples of what the others could be doing, not only through PPAs, but by whatever means the local-to-federal/tribal dynamic has to offer in support of environmental justice. tribal and environmental justice communities welcome and appreciate viewing their efforts displayed on the government websites highlighting successful partnerships and projects with states and EPA.

Memoranda of Agreement/Understanding (MOA/MOU) are equally important tools, but serve a different purpose compared to PPAs. The MOUs are legally binding, holding states fiscally and administratively accountable to do what they are authorized and funded to do – implement the federal laws. Following the money, this is where EPA and the states, tribes, and regulated entities in receipt of federal funding are clearly tied to Title VI of the Civil Rights Act, among other things. MOUs are also tied to EPA's budget tracking procedures. For this discussion, "agreements" and "understandings" are considered synonymous; the term "MOU" is interchangeable for either agreement.

MOUs do not typically include public review and comment, and they cover varying periods of time. However, in the spirit of this report, they are nonetheless important tools for EPA to recognize and use. MOUs ensure states are conducting (among other things) permitting-related duties according to the law. Although states may have 'primacy' to carry out the federal statutes, EPA controls the 'purse-strings' through the MOUs. EPA has an obligation to hold states accountable for all required elements of the authorized duties, processes, etc. This relates to the *Memorandum on EPA Statutory and Regulatory Authorities Under Which Environmental Justice May Be Addressed in Permitting - authored by then EPA General Counsel G. Guzy,* and dated December 1, 2000. The Guzy memo outlined many legally appropriate tools, authorizations, references, etc., where environmental justice is linked to federal environmental laws. These links connect to the states and tribes that are delegated or authorized and funded to implement those laws through the MOUs.

Further, there is nothing that should prohibit specific references within MOUs to remind federal fund recipients that they will be held accountable to support environmental justice efforts, procedures, PPAs, etc. This suggests a process that could be folded in over time as MOUs are renegotiated around the country. This also implies EPA needs to be ready to work with federal fund recipients if environmental justice obligations are not carried out according to the laws and the MOUs.

Occasionally, MOUs can be utilized as an alternative path to speed up pollution reduction either at specific sites or even at a larger regional and national scale. However, they can also be used by the business or industry to avoid rule making or postpone implementation schedules. Hence, the pros and cons of each MOU (if not the document itself) must be evaluated thoroughly, in an open public process that includes all stakeholders including representatives from businesses and local and tribal governments. The debate and controversy surrounding the railroad MOU with the California Air Resources Board serves as an example of mistakes to avoid and the process that should be followed prior to signing an MOU. The following links provide more background on environmental justice issues in California related to MOUs:

- http://www.aqmd.gov/news1/2005/AQMDResponsetoCARBMOU.html
- http://www.arb.ca.gov/msprog/offroad/loco/062405qarymou.pdf
- http://www.reportingonhealth.org/fellowships/projects/health-and-air-pollution-commerce
- http://cityclerk.lacity.org/lacityclerkconnect/index.cfm?fa=vcfi.dsp_CFMS_Report&rptid=99&cfnumber=05-0002-S152

Recommendations:

30. Include appropriate environmental justice-oriented language in its MOUs with states and tribes.
31. Ensure appropriate environmental justice language is clearly defined and built into those MOUs If MOUs are developed between EPA and other federal agencies.
32. Hold the authorized or delegated entities to a higher requirement of environmental justice engagement when discussing and negotiating MOU renewals.
33. Nationally, Hold regional EPA offices accountable to include environmental justice language and references in the regionally-negotiated MOUs.
34. Provide training to all EPA regional offices on the value of establishing relationships through meaningful communication with environmental justice communities and tribal nations. The training should include how to define and incorporate environmental justice into MOUs and PPAs.
35. Provide clear guidance to all federal fund recipients pointing out environmental justice references, procedures and obligations tied to the receipt and use of the funds.
36. Review and consider better ways to ensure 40 C.F.R. 124 (cited elsewhere in this report) is applied to the public participation processes carried out by primacy entities.
37. Review how states are incorporating the public participation process. To ensure meaningful public participation, the public notice and outreach process must include direct communication in appropriate languages through telephone calls and mailings to environmental justice and tribal communities, press releases, radio announcements, electronic and regular mail, website postings and the posting of signs (where local zoning laws may also apply for example).
38. Expand other forms of communication (see above) to notify the public of PPAs, permit hearings,

environmental justice meetings, etc. Notification of the public by publishing in the legal section of regional newspapers is antiquated and ineffective. This method should not be counted on to communicate, even if legally required.

39. Establish procedures for MOU completion to ensure all related environmental justice impacts are addressed through satisfactory negotiations between all parties *before* the agreements are signed.

5.0   CONCLUSION

The NEJAC appreciates the opportunity to provide input and has endeavored to meet EPA's timeline. We must make clear, however, that well-founded, true consensus advice takes more time and dialogue than this exercise afforded. Our Subgroup operated under time constraints very different from those experienced by previous Work Groups. Nonetheless, we were able to raise pertinent issues and affirm the usefulness of specific guidance given by our predecessor Councils. This process reminded us that the deliberative process in which NEJAC historically has engaged has long-term value to the Agency in seeking to implement environmental justice throughout its programs. We urge EPA to allow the NEJAC adequate time, access to relevant EPA experts, and resources to tackle complex questions. This support would allow the Council to make the consensus recommendations to help EPA lay the foundation for a future in which its permitting programs are keystones in continual progress toward environmental justice in this country.

Further, as was discussed at the July NEJAC meeting, EPA is considering creating an internal Agency work group to drill down on the actual process of delineating how to integrate environmental justice into the Agency's permitting practice and procedures. We recommend that EPA consider inviting NEJAC representatives and other non-agency experts to this work group. We envision a process much like the past NEJAC subcommittee structure where EPA staff worked side-by-side with NEJAC members and other outside representatives and experts on a range of issues and concerns. We think that this approach could yield a more comprehensive examination of permitting issues, and provide the Agency with a range of expertise to draw on in its further deliberations.

APPENDIX A

INCORPORATING ENVIRONMENTAL JUSTICE CONCERNS INTO PERMITS UNDER FEDERAL ENVIRONMENTAL LAWS

CHARGE
JULY 27, 2010

EPA seeks advice and recommendations from the National Environmental Justice Advisory Council (NEJAC) to inform how we can better incorporate environmental justice concerns into government decisions on permits issued under the Agency's various regulatory programs.

BACKGROUND

Importance of Permits: Permits are key to delivering environmental results in communities. Federal environmental statutes rely heavily on permits to deliver the environmental protection results that are the goal of our federal environmental laws. For example, the Resource Conservation and Recovery Act (RCRA) relies on permits to ensure that hazardous waste treatment, storage, and disposal facilities take effective measures to protect the surrounding community from exposure to the hazardous waste handled at those facilities. The Clean Water Act relies on permits to control discharges of pollutants into surface waters to protect water quality and communities' health and welfare. The Clean Air Act uses permits to restrict emissions of air pollutants from facilities to ensure that air quality standards are met and public health is protected from air pollution. These permits are a key to providing effective protection of public health and the environment in communities, given their role in addressing exposure to pollution and preventing adverse environmental and public health impacts. It is also important to recognize that each permitting process is governed by regulations, which vary from program to program. Moreover, considering environmental justice issues when developing rules is essential to effectively addressing them within permits.

Prior NEJAC Advice and EPA Actions: The NEJAC has addressed the role of environmental justice in the permitting process previously. In July 2000 the NEJAC issued a report entitled "Environmental Justice in the Permitting Process." In December 2000 EPA's Office of General Counsel issued a memo entitled "EPA Statutory and Regulatory Authorities Under Which Environmental Justice Issues May be Addressed in Permitting."[13] That memo concluded that EPA has legal authority to address environmental justice concerns in the permitting processes under several programs. Building on this foundation, EPA now wants to take action to better incorporate environmental justice concerns into the government's decision-making on permits.

Role of State and Local Governments: Federal environmental laws assign EPA with the responsibility of administering permitting programs and also authorize EPA to delegate these programs to states and tribes. Most of the permits implementing the federal environmental laws are issued by states or tribal governments, once EPA approves or authorizes the state or tribal program. EPA remains responsible for oversight of federal programs that are delegated to states and also has limited authority to review, comment, or object to state-issued permits. There are practical implementation constraints. For example, the volume of permits is much too high to enable EPA to be actively engaged in reviewing every state permit. In addition, many environmental permits, or other relevant decisions such as siting, that are important to communities are authorized under state law and issued by state or local authorities, with little or no federal involvement. Ultimately, EPA seeks to provide oversight of state programs in a manner that advances shared responsibility with states in order to fulfill Congressional mandates. This joint federal and state role, with local involvement in some cases, requires that EPA and states or tribes work together to exercise their authorities to ensure that environmental justice is taken into consideration into permitting processes as much as possible.

Role of Other Federal Agencies: Some of the federal permits that can affect the environment and the health of communities are issued by federal agencies other than EPA. While EPA has authority to review some permits

---

[13] See: http://www.epa.gov/environmentaljustice/resources/policy/ej_permitting_authorities_memo_120100.pdf

issued by other agencies, the primary responsibility for reviewing applications and deciding whether to grant a permit and on what terms and conditions lies with the lead federal agency. For example, Clean Water Act permits for filling wetlands or waters, which can affect communities in some areas, are issued by the U.S. Army Corps of Engineers (e.g., in Appalachia).

Role of Tribal Government: Some of the permits implementing the federal environmental laws can be issued by tribes, once EPA approves or authorizes the tribal program. Most environmental permits on tribal lands are currently issued by EPA. EPA retains some ability to review, comment, or object to tribal-issued permits, but this ability is limited both by law and by practical implementation constraints. In addition, some of the environmental permits that are important to communities are authorized under tribal environmental codes, with little or no federal involvement.

EPA's Goals: EPA wants to improve the government's ability to take environmental justice concerns into consideration in environmental permitting processes, whether permits are issued by EPA, other federal agencies, states, or tribal governments. One important way that EPA is working toward this goal is by incorporating environmental justice into federal regulations, which provide the foundation for permitting decisions. We also want to ensure that environmental justice concerns have received full consideration in the government's final decisions on the issuance and terms of the permits that implement federal environmental laws. To achieve its goals, EPA recognizes the importance of giving full consideration to environmental justice as soon as possible in government's permitting process prior to its final decision (e.g., draft permit phase, general permit issuance). We also want to ensure that communities have meaningful opportunities to obtain and provide information and to have their voices heard in the permitting process at the earliest point possible.

Opportunities and Challenges: EPA recognizes that the opportunities to consider environmental justice concerns in permitting decisions vary with the statutes and regulations underlying each permitting program. Based on these authorities, the range of opportunities is related to the types of permit decisions being considered. For example, there may be different opportunities to incorporate environmental justice concerns into a permit reflecting a technology-based performance standard as compared to a permit reflecting a harm-based standard. Or, opportunities may differ based on whether a permit addresses a specialized jurisdiction (e.g., wetlands) or a concentration of pollutants (e.g., non-attainment area). Finally, there could be differences based on whether a permit is to begin a new activity (e.g., construction of a new source of emissions) or to continue engaging in an ongoing activity (e.g., operation permit for an existing facility).

We are mindful that some programs may pose more challenges than others in this respect. One of the most difficult challenges, but one of the most important opportunities to reduce pollution in overburdened communities, is determining how to consider and address cumulative impacts where a number of different pollution sources affect a community. In light of the potential benefit from addressing cumulative impacts more effectively, we believe that our efforts to incorporate environmental justice concerns into permitting should focus first on those permit regulations and programs that are most conducive to considering environmental justice issues and cumulative impacts.

NEJAC's Role: We would like the NEJAC's advice on identifying the permit programs that we should address first in our efforts to incorporate environmental justice concerns. We think we can make the most progress by working simultaneously on two fronts: 1) identifying permit processes that provide the best current opportunities for taking environmental justice concerns into consideration within EPA-issued permits; and 2) working with states, the advocacy community, businesses and others to create a structure where cumulative impacts are routinely considered in permits issued by various levels of government that have the greatest potential to affect human health. We expect that trying to make progress on EPA-issued permits that have an immediate on-the-ground effect will help inform the necessary policy discussions about how to make institutional changes.

The two charges reflect this two-pronged approach. The first question seeks input on the types of permits we should work on under the first approach – EPA-issued permits. The second question invites your recommendations on types of permits that we should address with states and others to make more far reaching institutional change that includes consideration of cumulative impacts.

Next Steps: Our next steps will include reaching out to the states and Indian tribes, as well as federal agencies, who implement federal environmental laws. State environmental programs have long grappled with issues of environmental justice in permitting, and many have given considerable thought to the issues that we face. We are eager to begin sharing ideas and experience to improve our collective understanding, effectiveness, and consistency in taking action on this important issue.

THE CHARGE

EPA requests that the NEJAC provide advice and recommendations in response to the two questions below.

Question #1: What types of EPA-issued permits should we focus on now, to work on incorporating environmental justice concerns into EPA's permits?

We would like to focus on EPA-issued permits that are important to the public health and welfare of overburdened communities, and that have criteria and permit processes that provide the best current opportunities for taking environmental justice concerns into consideration in the permit decision-making process. We believe this approach will provide our best opportunity for making short-term progress and providing valuable lessons for further efforts. In providing your advice and recommendations, please consider:

(a) EPA permit types that are of the greatest concern and interest to communities with environmental justice challenges and environmental justice stakeholders;
(b) EPA permit types that are of the greatest importance in protecting the health and welfare of minority, low-income, and tribal communities; and
(c) EPA permit types that seem best able, based on the nature of the activity being permitted, how its impacts are distributed, how permits can be used to manage those impacts, and other considerations, to incorporate environmental justice concerns into permit decision-making in the near term.

Question #2: What types of permits issued pursuant to federal environmental laws, whether they are federal, state, or tribal permits, are best suited for exploring and addressing the complex issue of cumulative impacts from exposure to multiple sources and existing conditions that are critical to the effective consideration of environmental justice in permitting?

We recognize that a number of complex and challenging issues must be resolved to achieve our goal of meaningfully and consistently considering environmental justice in permit decision-making. Perhaps most critical is the issue of whether and how cumulative impacts from many sources should be taken into consideration in a permitting process. Permit decision-making typically focuses on individual sources of pollution, e.g., air emissions from a certain facility.

Yet, overburdened communities often experience cumulative impacts on their health and welfare from pollution from many sources at the same time, in addition to the existing stresses on health and welfare from other factors affecting these communities, such as poverty or health disparities. It is a challenge to understand whether and how these factors can be taken into consideration in deciding whether to issue a permit or what conditions to put in a permit for an individual source. For this part of the permitting work, we would like to identify permit types that best allow consideration of cumulative impacts, and that also help us design an approach for including consideration of cumulative impacts in programs for which states have primacy.

To begin our work on this issue, we would like to identify the federally authorized environmental permitting programs that provide the best opportunities for considering cumulative impacts in the decision-making process. We would like your advice and recommendations for identifying those programs.

Time Frame for Response: We would appreciate the NEJAC's response to the above questions within 60-90 days. As the Agency continues to work on the issue of environmental justice in permitting and other issues, we expect to bring additional requests to the NEJAC for advice and recommendations.

APPENDIX B

COUNCIL QUESTIONS RELATED TO EPA PERMITTING CHARGE

These questions are outlined for the purpose of ensuring clarity in our Subgroup's mission and proper scoping, as well as to assure that we understand EPA's fundamental goals in asking NEJAC's advice on how to consider environmental justice in permitting. The questions are asked in the spirit of offering practical, quality recommendations to EPA within the available period. Bulleted questions and variations on a thought are not mutually exclusive; a "yes" may be good for multiple interpretations on the Subgroup's part.

Threshold questions on EPA's goals and philosophy in looking at permits:

What policy goals should EPA consider as it goes forward in selecting permit types? \

- Whether the permits it selects and the approach it uses will be broadly applicable (beyond the initial subset of permit types selected)?
- Whether the states are likely to adopt the approach even if not mandated because it is workable?
- Whether the approach is likely to expedite or delay decision-making?
- Whether the community is likely to see tangible improvement in environmental quality and access to needed resources in a timely fashion? And in that context, whether EPA would also consider whether the permits and approach selected will have unintended adverse impacts on a local economy or jobs?

Questions Related to Question #1:
Several phrases in the charge questions could benefit from clarification.

"Types of EPA-issued permits"

- Is the charge to rank between the 'types' relative to the multiple federal acts for which EPA issues permits, e.g., Clean Air Act, Safe Drinking Water Act, RCRA, FIFRA, Clean Water Act, etc., (and/or specific subparts within these statutes)?
- Or is there some other 'type' of permit category we should be addressing (outside of Charge Question #2) – for example, self-implementing permits by rule vs. permits specifically negotiated by EPA (or a delegated state)?
- Could 'type' include those that are most contentious to environmental justice communities (regardless of statutory derivation), or most challenging for EPA in the context of attaining environmental justice in the community?
- Does EPA want to begin with facilities where relatively simple new practices can achieve positive results, or does it want to begin with the most difficult, controversial sites in order to build experience solving the most intractable problems?
- Should EPA begin with facilities to which environmental justice analyses in some form already have been applied (hazardous waste landfills, large chemical plants like Shintec, federal facilities), or start with a clean slate? If the former, have there been any successes such that EPA has a sense it understands best practices in incorporating environmental justice in permits?

"Focus on now" – as opposed to... later?

- The 'now' implies timing. Is the charge asking to rank types of permits to be addressed in a chronological order?
- Or does this imply *only focus on one or two types*?
- Is the thought to try to see results in the communities within the next two years?
- Is the purpose of the question to help EPA prioritize permitting resources? Paraphrasing, are you asking, "Where should we start?" suggesting *all permit types* will eventually see EPA's focused attention on environmental justice-related matters?

"Of the **greatest** concern and interest to communities" -- How can this be gauged?

- Complaints/lawsuits? Most vocal? Number of mentions by the public in NEJAC or other forums? A list that NEJAC – or EPA personnel -- would compile and recommend? Those determined by a new public participation process conducted specifically to compile such a list? Most confusing/complex types of permits?
- Most adverse? Determined by level or volume of contaminants, level of control assured at compliant facilities, reliability of compliance assurance, number of people potentially exposed, number of members of vulnerable populations exposed?
- Should EPA focus on facilities with multiple permits (for broad authority), only one permit (for ease of implementation), or no permit at all (because these are the environmental justice concerns about which communities have the least information and EPA no control)?

Short of statistics or surveys, the Subgroup feels this can really only be addressed by collective experience, and we feel short on sufficient data to address this criteria.

"EPA permit types that seem **best able**.... to incorporate EJ concerns into permit decision-making in the near term." Looking for clarifications on the emphasized terms:

- "Best Able" – Per the Guzy memo, there are multiple references to EPA's ability and authority to engage in environmental justice considerations and appropriate actions. Thus, does the question ask, 'Where should EPA **more fully exercise** such authorities?
- Or does 'best able' imply making the biggest positive difference sooner than later – perhaps at a greater cost, commitment, and political expense?
- Should EPA begin with the permits that already have the broadest public participation requirements, or the least?

"To incorporate EJ concerns into **permit decision-making** in the **near term**."

Respectfully, this is an oxymoron. Permitting is more often than not a longer-term process, from the application to review, hearings, issuance, oversight, enforcement, modifications, renewals, and in many cases, ultimate closure and clean-up. "Near term" doesn't synchronize well with this string of time consuming (often years), permit-related decisions for each one of the noted processes.
The Subgroup's presumption is that the question's consideration may include any or all of these steps. Please clarify if this is not EPA's intention in the question.

Questions Related to Question #2

"Best suited for exploring and addressing the complex issue of **cumulative impacts** from exposure to **multiple sources** and **existing conditions** that are critical to the effective consideration of environmental justice in **permitting**."

- These highlighted terms, factors, and considerations are very complex in relation to permitting. As noted in the previous set of questions regarding near term decision-making, should all aspects of "permitting" be considered? Please confirm.

Understanding the nature of "**overburdened communities, cumulative impacts, exposures to multiple sources**, and **existing conditions**."

- By these criteria, one must look above the fray of new, individual permits to a larger context. Rather, EPA and all involved stakeholders have to address the collective implications, which individual permits are not established to do. Thus, the question seems to be looking down an impractical path. Should EPA focus on permit categories, or should it instead use a screening tool to identify the communities with the highest level of environmental justice concerns, and then have a template to engage the community and use permits and other authorities to make progress toward environmental justice?

- In the concept of a 'total maximum daily loads' for a given water body (TMDLs - such as is in the Clean Water Act), the question is what's the 'total load' an entire community can safely, sustainably take on or absorb? Going over that load or capacity – implying the combined environmental loading from all forms of permitted pollution in an environmental justice community -- is the problem, particularly for the weakest members of the community. All governmental entities involved with any or all steps of permitting in such communities have to work on this together – along with all the permittees and community stakeholders and with those involved with the cleanup of existing sources of contamination. "Types" of permits does not get to this bigger-picture dynamic.

- If the cumulative risk approach is considered instead of the focus on sets of permits, does this suggest newly invigorated Interagency Working Group on Environmental Justice could provide new opportunities to achieve the goals NEJAC was seeking in its report on cumulative risk? Should this opportunity be considered in mapping EPA's objectives in permitting?

- Given these considerations, the Subgroup finds question 2 (and probably question 1, since it is the initial step in a project that includes the concepts raised in question 2) somewhat misdirected. These considerations are much better addressed in the NEJAC recommendations on cumulative impacts, compared to what this Subgroup can address in this short time frame. See: Ensuring Risk Reduction in Communities with Multiple Stressors: Environmental Justice and Cumulative Risks/Impacts (PDF) - December 2004.

- Could we enhance that body of knowledge in the next four weeks? More likely, the Subgroup will have to defer to a better-formulated NEJAC work group to fully tackle this question.

APPENDIX C

PRELIMINARY SURVEY OF ENVIRONMENTAL JUSTICE
CONCERNS AND PERMITS

This Appendix identifies facilities and activities of environmental concern mentioned in NEJAC reports, public meetings, and discussions; and the regulatory programs that may be used to address the concerns.

Kinds of Permits EPA Issues or Oversees in their Programmatic Implementation by States

Note that each environmental program/statute – New Source Review (NSR) and Prevention of Significant Deterioration (PSD), and Title VI under the Clean Air Act; Subtitles C and D under the Resource Conservation and Recovery Act (RCRA); National Pollutant Discharge and Elimination System (NPDES) under the Clean Water Act; Underground Injection Control (UIC) under the Safe Drinking Water Act; Toxic Substances Control Act; etc. – is associated with a number. The list of activities raising environmental concerns is likewise associated with number(s), as applicable, to show which concerns appear to be addressed under which environmental program/statute. For some environmental concerns, the environmental justice concern is only addressed for specific activities that require a permit. The concern will not be addressed with other activities creating a similar impact.

EPA Program	Total number of facilities permitted under program / number of permits [to be completed by EPA]	Total number of facilities EPA permits / number of permits in programs EPA oversees [to be completed by EPA]
NSR, PSD, Title V Clean Air Act (1)	NSR PSD Title V	
RCRA Subtitles C & D (2)	Subtitle C Subtitle D	
NPDES, 404 Clean Water Act (3)	NPDES 404	
UIC Safe Drinking Water Act (4)	Underground injection wells	
PCBs, chemical registration TSCA (5)	PCB cleanup Chemical registration Lead Asbestos	

Abandoned tires
Agricultural runoff
Air toxics (1)
Ambient tobacco smoke
Asbestos (2, 5)
Asthma triggers (1)
Asphalt plants
Auto body shops
Availability of clean water
Beneficial use/ recycling
Brownfields
Bus depots
Bus/vehicle idling
CAFOs
Cement plants
Chemical fires
Chemical plants (1, 2, 3)
Chemical use disclosure
Coal combustion residuals
Carbon sequestration units
Composting
Compressor stations (1)
Congestion
Construction and demolition facilities
Cumulative impacts/ risks (only for RCRA Subtitle C waste combustors) (1, 2)
Destruction of tribal artifacts and historically significant site (only for RCRA Subtitle C facilities) (2)
Diesel emissions
Dioxin (only for RCRA facilities, waste combustors) (1, 2)
Drinking water drawdown
Drinking water quality (3, 4)
Dry cleaners
Dust (for RCRA facilities) (2)
Exempt facilities (because of size or other exclusion) in single or combination
Facility location restrictions (only for RCRA, NPDES) (2, 3)
Fish contamination
Flares
Fracking
Fuel storage
Gentrification
Glycol dehydration facilities
Goods movement
Greenhouse gases

Green space
Hazardous waste generators (2)
Hazardous waste reclaimers
Hazardous waste treatment, storage and disposal facilities (1, 2, 3)
Hazardous waste incinerators (1, 2)
Household hazardous waste (2)
Industrial waste management
Land use planning procedures
Lead (only for RCRA facilities, water discharges, and stacks) (1, 2, 3, 5)
Light pollution
Litter/illegal dumping (2)
Manufacturing facilities (1, 2, 3)
Medical waste combustors (1)
Mercury (only for RCRA facilities, water discharges, stacks) (1, 2, 3)
Military ordinance
Mining operations
Mining waste
Mountain top mining
Municipal waste landfills (1, 2, 3)
Municipal waste recycling
Natural gas operation
Natural occurring metals in water
New source review alternative sites (1)
Noise
Odor (municipal waste landfills only) (2)
Oil and gas exploration sites
Oil waste
Open dumps (2)
Other cleanup projects (for Superfund, RCRA) (2)
Ozone (1)
Particulate matter (1)
PCB exposure (5)
Pesticide application and drift
Pests (only for RCRA municipal waste landfills) (2)
Plant upsets (1)
Printing plant emissions
Proximity of pollution to schools (only for RCRA facilities) (2)
PSD alternative sites (1)
Radioactive waste
Raw sewage/sewage overflow
Recyclers
Refineries (1)
Refinery waste
Resource Recovery Facilities
Rodenticide application
Salt piles
Scrap recyclers
Sewage sludge application (3)
Sewage treatment facilities (3)
Ship and boat emissions

Site selection/ review of alternatives
Smart Growth
Soil staging
Spills (3)
Storm debris
Sugar harvesting and burning
Superfund sites (2)
Surface runoff (3)
Traffic hazards
Transportation application of herbicides
Transportation corridors
TRI emitters (only if otherwise have permit)
Truck routing

Underground tanks (2)
Underground injection wells (4)
Urban farming
Utilities (1)
Vacant lots
Volume reduction facilities
Warehouses
Waste combustion (1, 2)
Waste transfer stations
Wastewater treatment facilities (2)
Water discharges (3)
Zoning authorizations

www.ingramcontent.com/pod-product-compliance
Lightning Source LLC
Chambersburg PA
CBHW080931290526
45795CB00007BA/2704